CW01500261

DISCLAIMER

The information contained in **"THE YOUNG ENTREPRENEUR MINDSET: The Skills Needed To Excel In Business,"** and its components, is meant to serve as a comprehensive collection of strategies that the author of this Book has done research about. Summaries, strategies, tips, and tricks are only recommendations by the author, and reading this Book will not guarantee that one's results will exactly mirror the author's results.

The author of this Book has made all reasonable effort to provide current and accurate information for the readers of this Book. The author and its associates will not be held liable for any unintentional errors or omissions that may be found.

The material in the Book may include information by third parties. Third party materials comprise of opinions expressed by their owners. As such, the author of this Book does not assume responsibility or liability for any third party material or opinions.

The publication of third party material does not constitute the author's guarantee of any information, products, services, or opinions contained within third party material. Use of third party material does not guarantee that your results will mirror our results. Publication of such third party material is simply a recommendation and expression of the author's own opinion of that material.

Whether because of the progression of the Internet, or the unforeseen changes in company policy and editorial submission guidelines, what is stated as fact at the time of this writing may become outdated or inapplicable later.

This Book is copyright ©2017 by **Raheim Young & Shannel Morris** with all rights reserved. It is illegal to redistribute, copy, or create derivative works from this Book whole or in parts. No parts of this report may be reproduced or retransmitted in any form whatsoever without the written, expressed and signed permission of the author.

Table of Contents

INTRODUCTION

Thank you for buying this fantastic guide— **"THE YOUNG ENTREPRENEUR MINDSET: The Skills You Need To Excel In Business."**

So, you want to start your own business? It can be overwhelming to start out in the world of entrepreneurship, especially if you are young. However, with a little business knowledge and research, anyone can succeed. The first step to becoming a successful young entrepreneur is to make sure you fully understand what you're getting into.

Most new entrepreneurs make the mistake of trying to do too much with very little. Of course, if you are just starting out, you must be excited about this new business venture; however, it is important to take a step back and carefully assess the situation. Any successful business comes with a business plan which the businessperson must stick to!

Over the course of your business journey, you will have to make minor adjustments along the way as you start to figure what works and what doesn't work for your particular situation, but the foundation of your business plan must always remain.

When formulating your business plan, you must first research the field you're planning on getting into. Find out what has worked for others and what has failed for them. Setting up meetings with successful young entrepreneurs in your area will also work wonders for two reasons:

First, you can pick their brains about their business plan to model yours after the parts of theirs that worked. Secondly, building relationships with other local business folks can only be a good thing for the success of your business.

As you start out with what will hopefully be a successful venture into the world of entrepreneurship, make sure your goals are defined, and in writing as well.

This business plan will not only keep you focused and productive going forward, it will also be instrumental in keeping you motivated as you have an outline for the path you are forging.

What is the main secret behind all successful entrepreneurs?

There is only one way to get the required motivation (driving force) for your business. In order to accomplish anything, you need a driving force; otherwise, nothing will happen. A wish is not strong enough to make you take action. Also, a dream is a weak desire and only a strong desire can drive you forward to act and accomplish your aims and goals. This is the reason why you need to know about the success stories of other entrepreneurs.

Reports have shown that motivation can change our mind for success. This is the main reason why some successful entrepreneurs keep talking about success mindset theory. What this means is that the moment you change your mindset to that of success, you will definitely get success.

Entrepreneur success stories can demonstrate to you about how reaching your target and achieving your goals may not be as far as it seems; it can even be as easy as setting the goals itself.

Let's Get Started!

BUSINESS SUCCESS TIPS FOR YOUNG ENTREPRENEURS

A company that is founded on the energy and enthusiasm of youths can give more extensive and established businesses a run for their money.

Young people have a lot of creative ideas to make money and plenty of free time to explore the many possibilities of making it work.

For most young people, the most prominent motivating factor for starting their own company is the flexibility of schedule that it offers, meaning that they can study and work on their terms.

In addition, the fewer financial responsibilities that are present at this time means that there is more money to put into the business.

You have the ideas but don't know how to implement them? Here are few tips to help you on your entrepreneurial journey.

❖ Believe in yourself

You may find very few sponsors that are willing to fund your business venture; this could be because of your age. Don't let it discourage you. Try different avenues and you could find help from the most unexpected quarters.

❖ Don't be afraid to ask for help

You'd be amazed at the amount of information and advice that is yours for the taking, only if you ask. Nobody knows what's on your mind unless you tell them. So, go ahead and tell your mentors and everybody else along the way about this fantastic business plan you have. People love to give advice and talk about things they are passionate about. If you come across the right person, the ideas and support you are bound to get could prove invaluable.

❖ Stay focused, but stay balanced too

Stay focused on your plan and look for every opportunity you get to network and promote your business. However, be careful so you do not overdo it. Earning a degree and starting a business side-by-side can be very intense. Making time to socialize and have other interests will go a long way in helping you avoid early burnout.

❖ Creative marketing is everything

Learn to use innovative marketing strategies to attract potential clients. Putting yourself in their shoes and thinking like them will give you a better idea of where to start.

Stay Motivated As An Entrepreneur

Aspiring entrepreneurs can easily get pumped up when starting a new venture, especially after reading about the numerous success stories of people who were previously in their position. The odds, however, are not always in one's favor.

Some young entrepreneurs face frustrations from time to time, and this can crush their aspirations in business.

Although some may argue that it's all about passion for the venture, the truth is that success does not come easy. You can expect to feel frustrations, tiredness, as well as the feeling of being in the wrong industry, but the aim is to stay committed and motivated. Self-motivation and encouragement to overcome a slump phase can be gotten in different ways. Here are some final tips:

❖ Schedule Appropriately

The organization ultimately leads to maximum productivity and is, therefore, the key to dealing with work-related stress. To avoid frustrations, you need to have your day planned out so that you feel in control. Scheduling helps you stay focused as you know in advance what you will be doing at a particular time. The schedule needs to be complemented by a deadline so that no item is postponed. You need to prioritize your work in a way that helps you focus on the essential tasks first.

❖ Set Sensible Goals

It is very crucial for you to remember why you started the business in the first place. Every venture needs to have a final goal which can be meditated upon. It is, however, essential to have short-term goals that are readily achievable and realistic. These will help you highlight your milestones and get the inspiration needed to push further. You may also want to avoid repetitive tasks, which are usually dull, by outsourcing some of them.

❖ Anticipate and Learn

A good entrepreneur always has a forecast of their venture as well as the expected glitches. Having an open mind to all possibilities will help you to quickly absorb, strategize, and recover from a mishap. Other than countering challenges, anticipation helps you assess your passion for knowing whether you are doing what you enjoy doing or just boring yourself. You also need to learn from your failures to avoid making a similar mistake again.

❖ Hunt for Ideas and Connections

Whenever you encounter terrible situations that cannot be solved by conventional solutions, try brainstorming for ideas. It is a form of positive thinking and it enables you to avoid frustrations.

You can also compile ideas from other sources such as books and the internet, filter and then implement them. Since entrepreneurs understand fellow entrepreneurs better, you need to join a mastermind group with like-minded people to get inspiration from their experiences.

❖ Reward Yourself

The fact that everybody needs a refresh once in a while is one of the most apparent tips.

As much as you may enjoy your long working hours, you need to take a break at some point to increase your awareness and delivery.

It is important that you take some time off during the week to engage in one of your hobbies and recharge your senses. A balanced life can be more gratifying as it helps you appreciate your business and its privileges.

BUSINESS MOTIVATION RULES YOU MUST KNOW

Business motivation is about motivating employees and customers alike. According to recent research, the organizations that are actively looking after the emotional well-being of their employees score better on the business motivation factor.

However, like every single concept or plan, motivation also involves some basic rules. Let's have a look at the ten business motivation rules that you must know:

❖ **Formulate an objective**

Formulating a purpose is the first rule of motivation before any further progress.

If a firm wants its employees to achieve higher levels of productivity and fetch them more revenues, it should first check how satisfied their employees are with the existing levels of motivation.

❖ Accomplish your aims

The second rule of business motivation is accomplishing your plans and objectives. You need to work on anything and everything that crosses your way. In business, nothing is too small or too big.

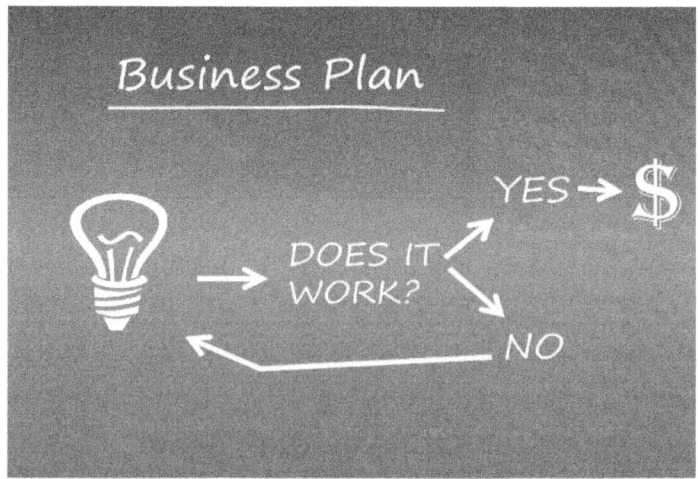

❖ Initiate discussions with like-minded people

When you mingle with people who have big ideas and high aspirations, you are likely to establish a positive attitude. You may as well create a business group to keep the spark of motivation ignited in both your heart and mind.

❖ Be eager to learn

The willingness to learn goes a long way in paving your path to business motivation. Once again, learning alone does not help you succeed. You need to apply in reality whatever you have determined in due course of time.

❖ Combine your talent with personal interest

It should be done in a way that helps you become empowered. For instance, if you like surfing the net, and your natural talent lies in writing, go ahead and enroll in some writing programs that will let you surf the net and earn some extra bucks by writing articles. Always remember, motivation is temporary but empowerment lingers around for a long while.

❖ Enhance knowledge that motivates

Reading a book can help you enhance your level of motivation. Sometimes, talking to people who share similar views on subjects of your interest can help you achieve business motivation.

❖ Never be afraid to take risks

Not being scared to fail is another rule of motivation. The more your fear of failure, the more you will lose your chance to succeed. So, take risks and remain motivated.

❖ Feel responsible

Take the onus and complete any task that is assigned to you. This will help you achieve higher levels of business motivation.

❖ Make your contribution meaningful

Whatever you do to keep the motivation levels at your workplace or business, make sure it pays in the long run rather than just fetch futile results.

❖ Don't monetize on motivation

Business motivation is not solely about money; there are a lot more factors involved. It helps you gain peace of mind while also helping you perform better at work. Of course, that involves monetary gains in the long run but not instantly.

YOUNG ENTREPRENEURS

What does it take to make it as a young entrepreneur? These principles can be applied to anyone who is searching for success, young or old; although this chapter will be focusing mainly on young entrepreneurs.

Intrinsic Motivation

Psychologically speaking, there are two types of motivation: extrinsic motivation and intrinsic motivation. Extrinsic motivation is when an external source prompts you to act. The best example of this would be the reaction you get when you place your hand on a hot stove. Your body is extrinsically motivated to **MOVE!**

Intrinsic motivation is entirely different. With original motivation, nothing forces you to act; your movement is of your own will and desire. It is often called "Self-Motivation." It is the type of motivation that successful young entrepreneurs possess.

You can begin to develop an intrinsically-motivated lifestyle today. All you have to do is to practice the act of doing things that are not prompted by external sources. This includes eating healthy, exercising, meditation, prayer, etc. The key is to perform an action for which there exists no motivation outside of yourself.

Self-Discipline

The second key goes along □uite nicely with the first. To reach your real potential as a young entrepreneur, or as an entrepreneur of any age, you must have a right amount of discipline in your life. The best kind of discipline is "self-discipline" because it combines the benefits of control with the practice of intrinsic motivation.

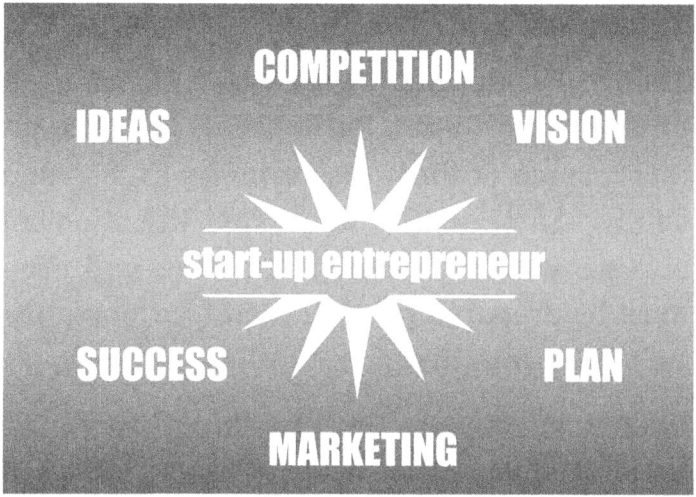

While intrinsic motivation is the practice of performing actions for which there are no external causes, discipline is the act of maintaining those activities.

What if you only filled your car with gas once all through the life of that vehicle? How far would you be able to go with it? A vehicle requires the repetitive action of adding fuel for it to go anywhere, just as an intrinsically-motivated young entrepreneur requires the repetition of successful activities to get where he or she wants to go.

Safeguard Your Dreams

Young entrepreneurs must safeguard their dreams. There are a lot of dream stealers out there. Some of them may even be friends and family. Some don't have the intention of hurting you, but sometimes, they will. You must be prepared for this; therefore, you must safeguard your dreams.

Do not let anyone tell you that "you can't," because this is not true. Surround yourself with positive and upbeat individuals who are likeminded and similarly focused.

If, for whatever reason, you're around people who are not, stay positive and stand up for your dreams.

Set Goals

Goal setting will be critical to your success as a young entrepreneur. You must always set goals for yourself, both large and small. Start by placing a large target, such as income, which you would like to achieve, then set smaller goals for yourself every now and then.

Small goals which lead to larger goals have proven to be effective in my own life. Sometimes, your lofty goal could take a few months or years to achieve, and you can get burned out and frustrated if you don't "achieve" anything before then.

Smaller goals between your larger ones will help keep your vision fresh and your body motivated.

Be A Leader

Being a young entrepreneur means being a leader. You are stepping out in faith and paving the way for yourself in the world.

People will naturally desire to follow alongside you—let them. You shouldn't develop a God complex, but you shouldn't belittle yourself either. Find a balance between the two. The most important thing is for you to know what you are worth.

YOUTH BUSINESS ENTREPRENEURS

Useful Tips

❖ **Who is a Youth Entrepreneur?**

A youth business entrepreneur is a passionate industrialist who produces specific, selected products and distributes them to consumers to make a handsome profit.

Youth entrepreneurs are usually more energetic, and therefore, they can take part in all the commercial activities of their entrepreneurship. They work hard to establish themselves from a very young age in the industrial sector.

The legitimate, acceptable age for youth business entrepreneurs to start any commerce is 16 years. The ideal time for youth entrepreneurs to undergo business training is during their academic term or when they are pursuing a degree or diploma.

Youth entrepreneurs must have a stable health since business activities are demanding and can hurt the health. They are also required to work for more extended hours in order to achieve the set objectives of the day.

Youth entrepreneurs need to supervise almost all business activities; hence, they have to be accessible at all times. They also need to prepare themselves to work and conclude the task efficiently and successfully.

Important Factors:

Entrepreneurs have to take a lot of risks if they wish to grow and establish themselves in the market. For this, it is vital for youth business entrepreneurs to prepare themselves mentally to make tough trade decisions.

To start with, entrepreneurs can examine the administration and technical support system of a couple of small business development centers and participate in special management programs. Several universities, colleges, and business schools around the globe conduct venture capital forums, youth business programs, and entrepreneurship seminars.

With the assistance of several collegiate entrepreneur associations, youth business entrepreneurs can educate themselves on myriad topics. Such partnerships can notify, encourage, and support business ideas of youths in order to mold them into successful capitalists of tomorrow.

Furthermore, they can also extend their commercial talent by surfing the internet. They can browse several sites devoted to tips and tricks and are related to youth entrepreneurship, to educate both the business and mind. Some sites also entail inspirational stories of successful young entrepreneurs to inspire upcoming youths.

Youth entrepreneurs can hone their skills for executing the business by undergoing training for manufacturing the goods, marketing, packaging, and managing excellent customer rapport.

Youth entrepreneurs need to march beyond the boundaries to achieve massive success in their industrial venture. Therefore, it is essential for them to gain knowledge through reading, experimenting, studying, and observing.

Entrepreneurs Believe In Themselves

When you speak to entrepreneurs, one thing you can be sure of is that they believe in themselves. Not discounting religion or faith at all, entrepreneurs do not always know exactly how things will turn out, but you can be sure they believe that they will be successful at whatever they do.

So why are successful entrepreneurs good at so many things? Because when they believe they can do something, they put their mind and energy into doing it.

An entrepreneur is very much like an athlete. A successful athlete wakes up early in the morning to go out for a run before most people hit the snooze button.

There is no doubt in the minds of athletes that they are in control of their bodies and there is no one who can beat them. Training and schooling usually go together, making the time needed for practice even more of a challenge. For professional athletes, the distraction of new found wealth and fame can be challenging as well.

So, the athletes focus on their sport and they always strive to be the best. Most athletes must have already selected a game or two in high school and subject themselves to rigorous training every day to improve their skills or reduce their time. It is a way of life which includes coaches and teams helping to keep them on track. Starting from a young age, there are camps and programs for every conceivable sport. You can excel in any event or team which considers your accomplishments to be worthy of inclusion.

The best athletes work hard to be the best they can be at one thing, while neglecting many other activities. Entrepreneurs work hard to be the best they can be; however, they do not have a support system or a team to hold them in line. There are no teams for the free spirit of the entrepreneur. Mom and dad did not take you out to the business library three times a week so that you could get on the entrepreneur team. There are no organizations for a young mogul. No summer camp for our little entrepreneur, but there are many for an eight-year- old future prima ballerina. Those camps are so busy that you get to meet several professional ballerinas. So, where does our young, prospective mega wealthy entrepreneur get started without a coaching staff at middle school?

The answer is that entrepreneurs become good at many things. Their desire to succeed does not only pertain to money. A true entrepreneur does not always know what field or business they will find themselves. It is true that many people start from a young age to follow a dream; they see the goal and try to build on it, giving 110% until reality throws a boulder on them and says, "Try something else." So, the future entrepreneur finds opportunities and interests that they find fascinating. Exploring a situation thoroughly is never a small undertaking. Like the athlete, these are highly-driven, highly-talented, and motivated individuals who want to succeed at everything they try. They just have not found what they will achieve due to a lack of similar structure which guides the athlete's world.

Entrepreneurs try out different hobbies and sports, seeking greatness only to come up short more often than not. So, they go off to school where they can impress the staff as the hardest workers and most dedicated students, or where they end up barely graduating because they just were not interested in anything enough to give a damn about the subjects being taught.

Entrepreneur And Talents

So, now the entrepreneur has many talents and is quite a convincing salesperson who is endowed with charm and wit that they usually give others a sense of confidence in their ability.

Everywhere you look, there are opportunities for the entrepreneur. Success and failure are like an athlete getting to the playoffs but not making the finals; however, there is no team to console or congratulate the entrepreneur. Family aside, an entrepreneur has no team. It can be lonely and hard to face defeat without knowing where to turn next.

This doesn't last long for an entrepreneur. No matter what happens, this is just another failure that makes the entrepreneur more capable in the future. A victory or a loss is merely another lesson to be learned and studied for the next endeavor. Like an athlete who wakes up after a significant defeat, an entrepreneur is still an entrepreneur the following day. Champions, however, can be made from athletes or entrepreneurs. The athlete that becomes a champion may not always have been a champion but was always an athlete. The entrepreneur will either win or lose but will still be a champion for having tried something new.

Giving your best every time and looking to find gold when no medals are being offered can be as difficult as training for a sport. Entrepreneurs believe in themselves; they see gold medals as the elusive brass ring to be sought after and won.

MYTHS ABOUT ENTREPRENEURS

The media has published lots of reports on entrepreneurs. Some are true, while others are not. Here are the five myths about entrepreneurs.

❖ **Myth #1: Entrepreneurs only care about making money**

A lot of people are of the opinion that entrepreneurs do what they do strictly for the money and that taking risks is all about the reward.

While fear of poverty or use of money as a scorecard may have some relevance and there are, of course, some entrepreneurs focused primarily on financial profits; generally, money is not the ultimate motivator for the majority of entrepreneurs.

Many successful entrepreneurs do not live a lavish lifestyle that reflects their financial success. Their motives are often more about ego and emotion. For most entrepreneurs, money is just a way to keep score.

Money is also a way to do more significant and exciting deals. The thrill of the challenge, the motivation of a new idea, and the risks involved have far more power to motivate the entrepreneurial spirit than money.

❖ Myth #2: Winning means somebody else is losing

You may have heard people speak of success in business as being "on the backs of others," suggesting that if an entrepreneur is winning, somebody else must be losing.

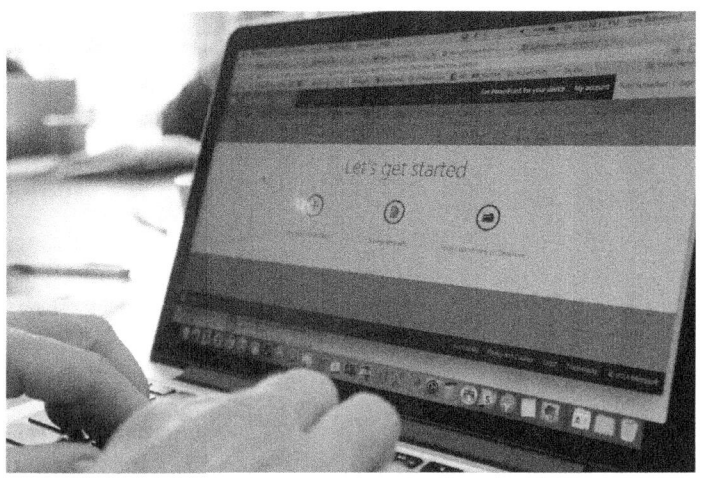

This attitude makes it seem like the only possible outcome from a business deal is to have one side win and the other side lose.

The resulting bottom line is zero. It is sometimes referred to as the "*zero-sum game.*"

Entrepreneurs are creative and expansionary thinkers.

Rather than accept a zero-sum result, and, contrary to the myth that an entrepreneur's success comes at the expense of others, entrepreneurs often try to figure out ways to make both sides win.

❖ Myth #3: The higher the risk, the higher the reward

This myth is always passed on to young entrepreneurs as a form of economic gospel. The theoretical relationship between risk and reward is coincidental at best, and only applicable in certain situations. The risk is a relative concept. All else being equal, real risks are modified by knowledge, experience, hard work, passion, and unforeseen circumstances. Applying knowledge to any investment can change the risk profile.

Equally crucial in considering risks, the perception of risks is often different from reality. What one person believes to be high risk might be a sure banker from another's perspective. Who then can say what a significant risk or a high reward is?

❖ Myth #4: As an entrepreneur, you can get rich quick

Have you heard of those dotcom millionaires? In the internet world, it sure seemed like people get rich overnight. But always remember that things often look more comfortable than they are. It may seem to you that entrepreneurs made enormous amount of money, but are you aware of the degree of hard work that was put in? Think twice about becoming an entrepreneur, if you think you can get rich quick.

❖ Myth #5: A good business plan is the entrepreneur's critical roadmap to success

Venture capitalists often make business plans the essential criteria in deciding whether or not to fund new companies.

Business educators often talk about business plans like they are the Holy Bible of business success. The theory is that the better and more complete the business plan, the higher the chance of success of that business. However, this is a myth.

While having an idea or a goal is critical, believing that you can create a structured and formal business plan that will endure time or place is merely naive. In the real world, it rarely happens.

SECRETS THAT SUCCESSFUL ENTREPRENEURS WON'T TELL YOU

Every entrepreneur is looking for that edge to help make their business a success. While there are a lot of successful entrepreneurs out there willing to give inspirational advice, few are eager to tell you the nitty-gritty truth that will help your business to be successful.

Having found a few successful entrepreneurs willing to share their struggles, here are some secrets that most successful entrepreneurs won't tell you.

You don't need to have breakthrough ideas, and you just need to execute any idea better than the competition. It is something that a lot of entrepreneurs get stuck on. New ideas are great, but if you can't follow through, it doesn't matter. Being flexible, adapting to the situation, and making old ideas better can be all you need to launch your business.

The key to success comes with failing, **A LOT**. Some of the best lessons you'll learn come with picking your face up off of the pavement and starting over, making sure you do things differently this time.

The road to success is a really long one. Success doesn't happen overnight (usually). Instead, it's a long and twisted path that sometimes seems to double back on itself. Perseverance and dedication will see you through.

You can't do it alone. This is especially true when you are starting out. You need a support network to keep you motivated, to spread the word of mouth, and to share your website and content. Once your business picks up, you need a dedicated team to help you take your dream to the next level.

Starting out in business involves a lot of begging. Without any track record or experience in the business, you'll have to work hard to convince people to give you a try and to invest in your company.

Sometimes, you have to fake it till you make it. It can mean letting your confidence get the best of you, convincing that prospective business client that you know all about X only to rush home to research it afterward to complete the job, and representing yourself a bit more grandly than you currently are to get where you need to be.

Even as a success, you'll still experience failure. Once the ball gets rolling, and you figure out what to do better, your successes become more monumental and your failures become smaller. However, you will still fail every single day.

Success brings extra stress, worry, and doubt. Every day is filled with the fear of that last business risk failing, of your company falling apart, or of losing everything and having to explain to your family that you're suddenly broke. These feelings can either cripple you or propel you forward.

Success is lonely. Sure, you may have some people that look up to you and admire your success, but at the end of the day, you're the one making all the final decisions. Therefore, the responsibility for any failure rests on you.

Top Fears Of Entrepreneurs

1. Fear of Failure: Without a doubt, an entrepreneur's biggest fear is failure. This is understandable because 95 percent of all businesses fail within the first five years. When you're starting with those kinds of odds, it's okay to be a little freaked out.

2. Economic Uncertainty: Five years ago, the economy may not have been a forefront concern for a startup entrepreneur. But today, businesses, both big and small, young and old, are worried about what the declining economy would mean for them.

3. Being your Boss: As a small business, especially when starting up, there's very little stability and security. Unlike traditional employment, you probably don't have an office, employees, benefits, or a paycheck. Ultimately, what you don't have is a boss, someone to guide you along.

4: Consuming Your Life: The idea of not having any time for yourself, neglecting your family , and giving up your social life can be terrifying.

5. Staying Afloat: You need money to start up, you need money to operate, and you need money to grow. Throw the dismal economy into the equation when people are spending less, when it's taking longer for small businesses to get paid, and when money is even harder to come by.

6. High-Wire with No Net: When you have been in your own small business and survived the early years that weed out most startups, you have the fear that you can never turn back to "the devil you knew" (i.e., traditional employment). The struggles of entrepreneurship make you forget why you left corporate America in the first place and your memories become revised to dwell on how comfortable and happy it all was "back then."

7. Losing Ground to the Jones': Even though your business may be getting more profitable every year, you look at your old car in the driveway and at the Jones' new Lexus and feel that if only you'd stuck to being a corporate (fill in the blank), you'd have new toys, too.

8. The Merry-Go-Round Stopping: Your business is cooking, but you worry that somehow, someday, and soon, the phones will go silent, and no one will want what you sell anymore.

9. Stuck in Third Gear: You know how to cruise at 40 MPH, but you need and want to do 90 (this is metaphorical). You fear never breaking through the wall of your business being merely "okay."

10. Emperor Has No Clothes: And the big-daddy of all entrepreneurial nightmares—you dream that you're walking down the street when you suddenly discover that you forgot to put your shorts on. Perhaps if you act natural, no one will notice. Lots of entrepreneurs think everyone else is smarter than they are and they live in fear of the world finding out their secret.

ENTREPRENEUR MINDSET TIPS

Discover Why You Need To Invest In Yourself

One of the most critical aspects of developing a business mindset is to invest in yourself. The only thing most people invest in themselves is food. We also have to invest in educating ourselves and growing in wisdom. Your education doesn't stop when you leave college.

One thing that schools and colleges don't teach you is **SUCCESS 101**. It is something the academic schools won't show you, and rather, it is developed internally.

Developing the fundamental attitudes and desires to succeed takes character, and it is not a spur of the moment decision or something you do because it sounds like a good idea.

The moment someone stops learning, they stop growing. There is no such thing as being stagnant because the world is continually advancing—anything that doesn't follow their direction will be left behind.

Unfortunately, this is what happens to people who leave college or university. They stop growing. Therefore, they start degrading. Their minds get atrophied and they lose their desire to learn.

Investing in ourselves also means that we learn new ways to acquire wealth. As your wealth grows, you will have more options to improve.

Learning to develop your wealth requires a confident attitude that most people had when they were young but lost along with their dreams when people tell them to stop.

They settle for mediocre lives and abandon the pursuit for success the moment they stop investing in themselves.

How does one develop the proper mindset and attitude? Does it require a lot of changes?

Yes and no. Change is required but not impossible.

The first thing you need to do is to be open to new teachings. It's just like a teacup; when a cup is full of water, you can't pour in anything. It won't go in, and it will overflow. So, what do we do if we need to get new water? First, just empty the cup by pouring the muddy water out of it, only then will you have the capacity to learn new things. The next thing you need to do is to learn from a mentor or a successful person. We need a guide and a direction; someone we can look up to and follow. Don't learn from negative people. Your beer buddies may be your lifelong friends, but they won't take you places.

Taking advice from them is suicidal. If you fall sick, you would rather see a doctor and not a car mechanic. In fact, you would want to see the best doctor there is! Not some crack doctor without any credibility.

The last attitude you must develop is an action habit. You can learn from all the gurus, read all the books, and attend all the seminars, but if you do not take action—massive action—you will be even worse off than when you just started, full of motivation, but no direction (leading to lots of frustration). Although this is the hardest part, it gets easier when you get started.

Boost Your Business Motivation Now

Great! We're in the perfect state for a motivation booster that will give our get- up-and-go an injection of zest and put us in the ideal frame of mind to push our businesses into a faster, fitter, and fresher phase.

Try this three-step process and see for yourself how quickly you start to feel inspired to move on up. Clear an hour in your desk diary, or do this at home instead of watching the soaps!

❖ Step One

Audit your successes: make a list of all the achievements you've had in your business up to this point.

They can be big or small achievements; just keeping your company afloat through the kind of economic storms we've had over the last year is a huge success; so, definitely put that on your list.

Winning a significant contract, plugging your way through a week of cold-calling, taking on your first staffer—any or all of these can also be on your success list.

Remind yourself how you felt at the time of the success and see if you can relive that feeling, that little spark of excitement or satisfaction.

❖ Step Two

Analyze your successes: how did your accomplishments happen? Luck? Unlikely! The Roman philosopher Seneca pronounced: "*Luck is what happens when preparation meets opportunity.*"

What preparations did you make when you previously felt lucky? What opportunities did you meet, greet, and grab with both hands?

What did you **DO** that brought success to your grasp the last time around? Work through your list, identify and note down at least one action that took you towards your achievement.

Add any circumstances that were in your favor, or factors that contributed to your success.

❖ Step Three

Study the actions you've identified and decide which **THREE** you can carry out over the next week and which **THREE** you can carry out in the longer term, say a month or during this quarter.

They may not be the same because time has passed, your situation is different, and the circumstances surrounding the actions have inevitably changed, but there is a way you can transfer the value of those actions and apply it to your present conditions.

Also look at the circumstances and contributing factors to your success and see if you can match them to your present situation somehow or if you can see how they may come together in future, and plan accordingly.

CONCLUSION

All in all, negative feelings are normal since we sometimes push too hard; hence, we tend to be stressed or feel down whenever we don't get the desired results. In such a case, you do not have to reevaluate your career or life goals, you only have to understand that it's part of life. You just need to strategize and adjust yourself to counter the side effects.

Business plans can be useful initial tools, but they should be used only as guidelines. Trial and error, luck, creativity, flexibility, and adapting to unforeseeable developments are ultimately what makes an entrepreneurial venture succeed.

If you want people to know and trust you as a young entrepreneur, then all your activities should reflect this. Be helpful to people who need help. By giving back to the online community, you gain far more in return. Try to gain a reputation as an honest and honorable business person.

Do not be put off if your current level of ability is not up to par. A lot of successful people have the less technical knowledge but are successful due to giving quality information to their readers and followers.

People won't support your business if they do not understand what you are about, so make sure you stick to your goals and focus your energy in a single direction.

Successful entrepreneurs know when to use creative problem-solving rather than general business plans. Do things each day that are going to increase your motivation for the business and lead to success. Eliminate stress and keep things simple. The more complicated things get, the more stressed out you will be, and stress can kill your motivation quickly.

Thank You Once Again For Buying This Fantastic Guide!

Printed in Great Britain
by Amazon

19487027R00038